The Caterpillar Waltz

Music and Lyrics by

Grant Brad Gerver

Illustrated and Collaged by

John and Kathy Harper

And a special thank you to Martha Brady
for her help and guidance   (JH / KH)

With Gratitude to My Son, Casey

Love, Brad Gerver

My red-haired

son

taught this to

me

You always put the caterpillar back on to the tree.

Oh caterpillar,

caterpillar

Don't wanna squish

you green

Just like me you deserve to live

To fly in the magic breeze, oh...

To fly in the mystic breeze, oh...

You do not
crush spiders
Have to let 'em
go free

You always pet
the dog
when he stands
at your knee

He does not like to fish

Cuz it hurts to

see them suffer

Could not stand to hunt

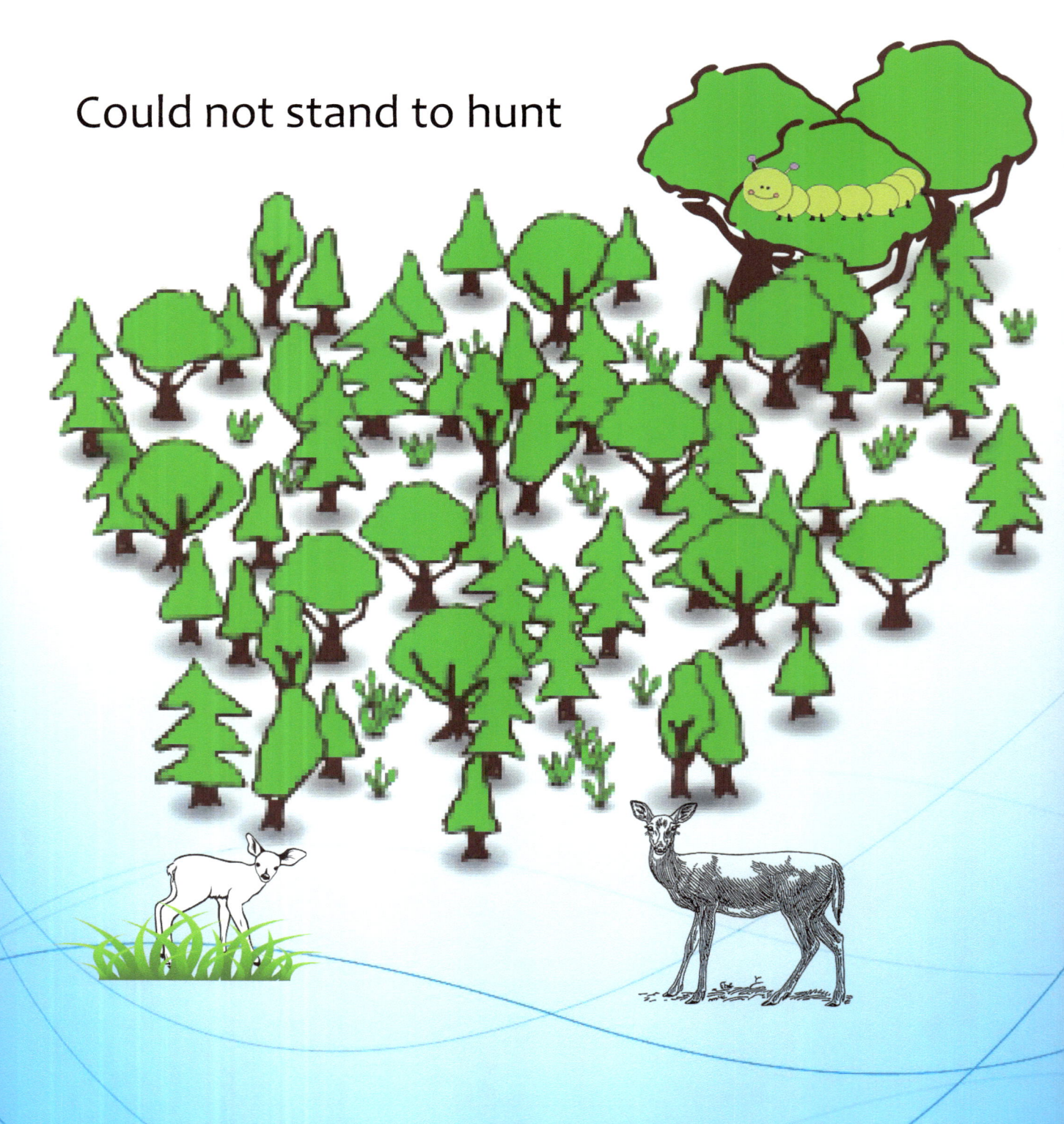

Cuz it might be

somebody's mother

He steps lightly upon his

Mother Earth

Not because we make him

but because it's in his heart

Here is what he

stands for

So naturally

You always put the caterpillar

Back onto the tree

Caterpillar

My red-haired son
Taught this to me
You always put the caterpillar
Back on to the tree

Oh caterpillar, caterpillar
Don't want to squish you green
Just like me you deserve to live
To fly in the magic breeze, oh
To fly in the mystic breeze

You do not crush spiders
Have to let 'em go free
You always pet the dog
When he stands at your knee

He does not like to fish
Cuz it hurts to see them suffer
Could not stand to hunt
Cuz it might be somebody's mother

He steps lightly
Upon Mother Earth
Not because we make him
But because it's in his heart

Here is what he stands for
So naturally
You always put the caterpillar
Back on to the tree

The Real Story of the Red-Headed Boy

My red-haired son and I were at Wheeler Park in Downtown Flagstaff, Arizona. After finishing our set at a music festival, my bandmate, Steve Rice and I chatted. At that moment, a caterpillar fell on my forearm. I gave it to my son, Casey Spike Gerver, and thought no more about it as Steve and I talked. Minutes later, my 6-year-old said, "Dad, I'll be right back." Out of the corner of my eye, I saw him placing that caterpillar back onto the giant elm tree from which it came. He stretched his small frame as high as he possibly could, on tiptoes. It greatly warmed my heart and speaks volumes of what he is all about to this very day. Caterpillar Waltz is completely true. The hundreds of times I have played it for kids and folks of every age, I am grateful for the jolt of joy it brings. ~ Grant Brad Gerver

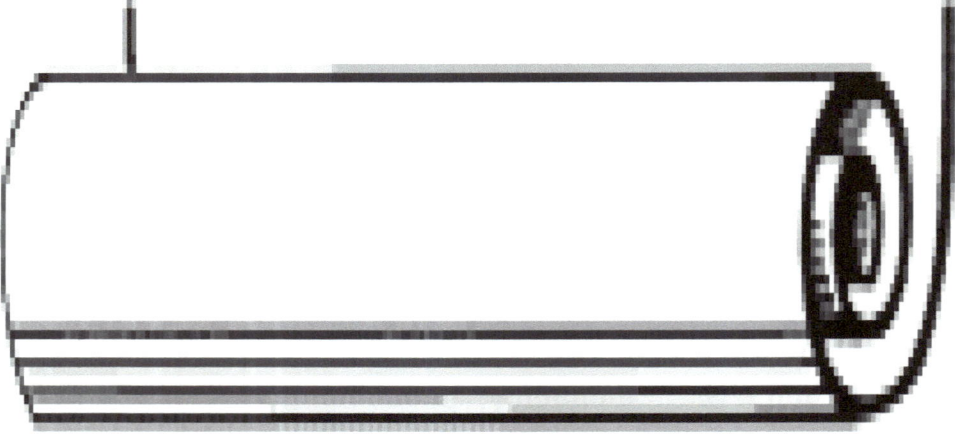

To Watch a Video of Grant Brad Gerver
performing this song, go to:

www.caterpillarwaltz.com

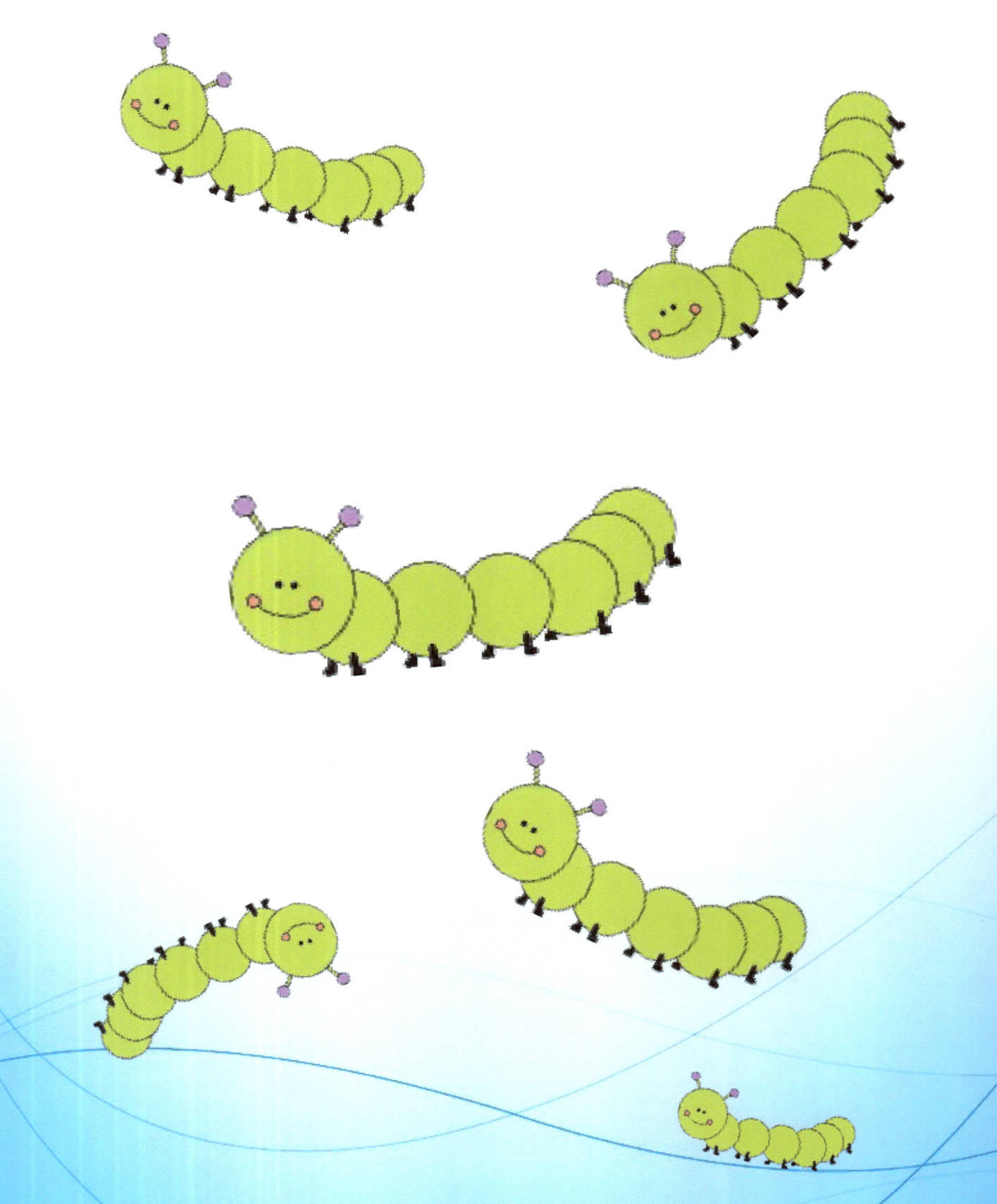

www.ingramcontent.com/pod-product-compliance
Lightning Source LLC
Chambersburg PA
CBHW060825290526
45792CB00005BB/1803